Exploring English 5

Literature Reader

Collins

Exploring English 5

Literature Reader

Sujata Aslam

Acknowledgements

The publishers have applied for permission for the following:

George Leslie Norris for *A Tiger in the Zoo;* Ruskin Bond for *A Lesson for the Teacher;* M. S. Mahadevan for *Sam Spook's Triumph*

Acknowledgments for these will be made in the future editions of the book.

Every effort has been made to trace copyright holders and to obtain their permission for the use of copyright material. The authors and publishers will gladly receive any information enabling them to rectify any error or omission in subsequent editions.

Published by Collins India

A division of HarperCollins*Publishers* India Private Limited

HarperCollins *Publishers*
A-75, Sector 57, Noida, Uttar Pradesh 201301, India
1 London Bridge Street, London, SE1 9GF, United Kingdom
2 Bloor Street East, Toronto, Ontario M4W 1A8, Canada
Lvl 13, 201 Elizabeth Street (PO Box A565, NSW, 1235), Sydney NSW 2000, Australia
195 Broadway, New York, NY 10007, USA

Browse the complete Collins catalogue at
www.collins.in

First edition 2016
Latest revised edition 2018

Reprint: 10 9 8 7 6 5 4 3 2 1

ISBN: 978-93-5136-870-0

Typesetting and page layout by Mammoth Studioz

Printed and bound by Nutech Print Services - India

PREFACE

Collins Exploring English is a multi-skill course in English, which adheres to the National Curriculum Framework guidelines, 2005.

The course is both educational and inspiring for children. Through its carefully designed structure and exercise, it aims to develop a love for English literature and equip students with skills to think critically and communicate effectively in a wide variety of contexts. It is also designed to widen students' horizons and knowledge, while fostering their enjoyment of reading and encouraging greater curiosity about the world beyond the classroom.

The course offers:

- a wide variety of meaningful topics and information-rich texts which motivate students and promote critical thinking whilst remaining age-appropriate
- a wide range of original and adapted texts, representative of both Indian and world literature, to encourage young learners to extend their reading skills
- materials from which students can develop as moral, thinking young people, and learn about the world around them
- cross-curricular topics, which students can relate to other subjects, such as science, geography, mathematics, and politics
- a syllabus designed to meet the latest CBSE curriculum framework
- carefully graded units to ensure clear progression through the grammar syllabus
- regular formative and summative assessment and help with exam preparation
- plenty of opportunities for communicative practice

Collins Exploring English is a multi-component course which includes coursebooks, workbooks and digital resources for all levels, as well as literature readers from level 3 onwards.

Literature Readers 3–8

The Literature Readers aim to develop in students an appreciation for the written word and an enjoyment of literature. The reading passages in each chapter offer a glimpse into diverse cultures and histories and show how language can be used to bring them alive.

Each chapter includes the following elements:

- An introduction: gives a short background to the reading passage, with questions to generate interest in the reader. For passages which are excerpts from well-known novels, the introduction contextualises the preceding events.
- Reading passage: carefully selected short stories, poems and extracts from classic novels from various periods and regions, as well as original plays.
- The passages cover various literary genres, such as biography, folk tale, lyric poetry and nonsense verse as well as tragedy and comedy. The genre is mentioned at the beginning of every chapter, while a reference list at the end of the book gives a brief explanation of each genre.
- Comprehension: comprises various types of factual, inferential and extrapolative exercises. Each chapter has a short, objective exercise which tests the student's close reading of the passage, and longer text-based questions which test their ability to understand and reproduce information in a coherent way, as well as analyse the text for deeper meaning.
- Vocabulary: tests the student's understanding of new words and their ability to use them contextually.
- Activity: includes a variety of writing tasks derived from the reading passages, such as letter and story writing as well as poster making, to be done individually or as part of a group.
- Literary terms: these identify and explain the way devices such as simile, metaphor, personification and irony are used within the reading passage. Students can also refer to the glossary of literary terms at the end of the book for the definition of each term.
- About the author: this short biography places the authors in the context of their time and mentions their well-known works for the interested reader to explore further.
- Suggestions for further reading: a short description of selected works by the same author or on the same topic as the reading passage, to encourage and foster a habit of reading.

Coursebooks 1–8

Coursebooks 1–5 comprise ten units, each based around a reading passage. There are also five poetry texts, spread throughout each level. In Coursebooks 6–8, each unit is based around a specific topic and includes two reading passages (a factual and a fictional piece) and a poem; comprehension, vocabulary and grammar exercises; and listening, speaking, writing and language skills activities. In addition, two Projects and two Life skills sections are provided at each level.

Workbooks 1–8

The workbooks provide additional material for skills practice, review and assessment. They include practice exercises on grammar, key vocabulary, language skills, reading and writing, as well as two assessment sections.

Digital resources

The Collins DigiSuite DVD comprises:

1. **Enhanced e-book:** this consists of the Coursebook in digital format with additional multimedia features and access to lesson plans, answer keys and worksheets.
2. **Test Generator:** an easy-to-use tool to help teachers create tests with a few clicks.
3. **Teacher Resources:** includes PDFs, lesson plans, answer keys, audioscripts, additional worksheets, further project ideas, and extra support with CCE assessment.

CONTENTS

1

The Milky Way

All tribes across the world have their own collection of stories and myths about how things came to be. The Milky Way is the galaxy in which our solar system exists. This legend offers an explanation about how the Milky Way was created.

A long time ago in the Cherokee country, there lived an old man and an old woman who **made their living** by beating **meal** and selling it to the other villagers for meat and skins.

Then one year, they noticed that someone had been stealing some of their meal at night. They were **alarmed** because they knew that none of the villagers would do this.

They looked around the house and then around the meal **pounding** place and finally found the **tracks** of a giant dog. When they looked at the tracks, they were scared because they had never seen such big animal footprints before.

make a living: When you **make a living**, you earn enough money to buy all the things you need.
meal: (here) A **meal** is the powder of any seed that is eaten, such as wheat or corn.
alarmed: To be **alarmed**, is to be afraid.
pound: When you **pound** something, you crush it into a powder.
tracks: Tracks are footprints left by an animal, human or vehicle.

They thought about the size of the tracks and discussed the theft of the meal all day, but couldn't decide what to do about it.

That night, the meal disappeared again. The next day, the old couple called a meeting with the villagers to decide what was to be done about the giant dog.

Everyone gave their opinion, but the old man **disapproved** of their methods because he was afraid of hurting the dog, who he believed was from another world.

At last, the old man said that the villagers must visit his house. They would all bring **noisemakers** so that they could scare the dog away.

And so it happened. Everyone went to the old couple's house and waited for the giant dog.

It was a starry night and the old man finally spotted the dog. It was approaching their house from the west.

He was a great dog and his coat shone silver in the moonlight.

When he came to the meal, he began to eat the meal in great **gulps**. The old man was scared, but he finally gave a shout as a signal and all the family rose and began making noise.

They shouted and shook their **rattles** and pounded their

disapproved: When you **disapprove** of something, you don't like it or disagree with it.
noisemaker: A **noisemaker** is an instrument that creates a loud noise and is used mainly during festivals.
gulp: (here) A **gulp** is the amount of food eaten in one bite.
rattle: A **rattle** is an instrument that makes short and sharp knocking sounds.

drums until the noise rolled up the mountain like a great thunder.[1]

The dog, hearing all this, got frightened and confused and ran round and round within the circle formed by the shouting people.

Then, he gave a great leap into the sky, and the meal poured out of his mouth making a white **trail** across the sky.

LITERARY TERM

[1] This is an example of a **simile**. The sound created by the noisemakers' drums and rattles has been compared to the sound of thunder.

This is where we can see the Milky Way. To this day, the Cherokee call it 'Gil'LiUtsun'yi', which means 'Where the dog ran'.

ABOUT THE ORIGIN OF THE STORY

Cherokee is pronounced 'Chair-uh-kee'. It comes from a word meaning 'speakers of another language'. The Cherokees are original residents of the southeast part of America. Storytelling is very important to the Cherokee Indian culture. There are many traditional Cherokee legends and fairy tales. Some famous Cherokee legends are about how the world was made, about thunder and eagle giving out powers to the animals, etc.

trail: A **trail** is a stream of dust, smoke and light left behind by something moving.

Comprehension

A. Say whether these sentences are true (T) or false (F).

1. The old couple made their living by selling salt.
2. One day, they found that someone was stealing their meal.
3. They discovered the tracks of a giant cow and were sure that the meal was being eaten by the cow.
4. They decided to bring noisemakers to drive away the giant animal which was stealing their produce.
5. The giant cow was seen approaching from the east.
6. The animal was huge in size and his coat shone like silver.
7. When the animal began to eat the meal, the villagers began making noise like a great thunder.
8. The cow ran away, frightened by the noise.
9. The dog leapt in the sky and the meal poured from his mouth, leaving behind a white trail.

B. Answer these questions.

1. What did the Cherokee people mainly eat?
2. How did they buy and sell things?
3. Why was the old couple sure that no one from their village was the thief? What does this tell us about their village?
4. Why were they alarmed when they saw the tracks of a dog?
5. How and what did they decide to stop the theft?
6. What is the Milky Way called by the Cherokee? How was it formed?
7. How would you have felt if you had seen the tracks of a giant animal near your home?

8. If an animal steals from you, would you kill the animal or use some other means to protect yourself and your property?

Vocabulary

A. Write the antonyms of the underlined words and rewrite the sentences using them.

1. She was clear about her future plans and how to achieve them.
2. She wore a bright red dress with matching shoes.
3. The floods did great damage to the crops.
4. The airplane disappeared into the clouds.
5. She heard a shout and turned around quickly.

B. Complete the crossword puzzle.

Across

3. not to like something
5. to take away something without the knowledge of the owner
8. a meeting
9. an instrument used to make sharp short sounds

Down

1. jump
2. very large
4. to come close
6. another word for autumn
7. a stick used to crush something

Activity

The Cherokee have an explanation of how the Milky Way was formed.

Make your own story about how the Milky Way was formed.

Draw an illustration to support your story.

SUGGESTIONS FOR FURTHER READING

- ***How the Rainbow was Made***: This is the story of Nanabozho, an Ojibway Indian, who sets out to paint the flowers in his meadow. While he is painting flowers in different colours, two bluebirds dip their wings in his pots of paint and spread streaks of vivid colours in the sky.
- ***How Corn Came to Be***: This is a story about two hungry boys who offer their dinner to a lady, who asked them for food, and remain hungry themselves. In return, they get 'Tanchi' or corn as a reward.

2

A Tiger in the Zoo

LESLIE NORRIS

The powerful and majestic tiger, used to roaming freely in the jungles, has been confined in a small cage. How do you think the king of the jungle feels?

He **stalks** in his vivid stripes
The few steps of his cage,
On **pads** of velvet quiet,
In his quiet rage.

He should be **lurking** in shadow,
Sliding through long grass
Near the water hole
Where plump deer pass.

He should be **snarling**[1] around houses
At the jungle's edge,
Baring his white fangs, his claws,
Terrorising the village!

But he's locked in a concrete cell,
His strength behind bars,
Stalking the length of his cage,
Ignoring visitors.

stalks: When you **stalk** something, you follow it closely without being seen or heard.

pads: (here) The soft parts under the paws of an animal are its **pads**.

lurking: When an animal **lurks**, it waits in a secret or hidden place, especially in order to hunt its prey.

snarling: When an animal **snarls**, it makes a loud noise while showing its teeth.

LITERARY TERM

[1] This is an example of **onomatopoeia** or sound word. 'Snarling' sounds similar to the threatening sound made by a tiger.

He hears the last voice at night,
The patrolling cars,
And stares with his brilliant eyes
At the **brilliant** stars.

brilliant: (here) Something that is **brilliant** shines brightly.

ABOUT THE POET

George Leslie Norris (1921-2006) wrote short stories and poems. His collections of stories, *Collected Stories*, and anthology of poems, *Collected Poems*, won numerous awards. Norris had started writing poems at the age of seven years. Besides being a poet, he was also a member of the Royal Air Force.

Comprehension

A. Answer the following questions in a few lines.

1. *He stalks in his vivid stripes*
   The few steps of his cage,
   On pads of velvet quiet,
   In his quiet rage.
   a. Where do you think the tiger is?
   b. Why does he take only a few steps?
   c. What does the phrase 'velvet quiet' refer to?
2. *But he's locked in a concrete cell,*
   His strength behind bars,
   Stalking the length of his cage,
   Ignoring visitors.
   a. Why do you think that the stanza begins with the word, 'But'?
   b. Explain the phrase, 'strength behind bars'.

3. *And stares with his brilliant eyes*

   At the brilliant stars.

   a. Who is staring at the 'brilliant stars'?

   b. Why have his eyes been described as 'brilliant'?

   c. Why does he stare at the 'brilliant stars'?
4. Briefly describe the tiger.
5. What are the two settings where the tiger has been described? What differences do you find between the two settings?
6. Where do you think the tiger would rather be?
7. Do you think the tiger is calm or angry? Give examples from the poem to support your answer.
8. How does this poem make you feel? Share your thoughts with the class.

The language of poetry

The poet uses certain words in the poem to describe the different movements of the tiger.

A. Quote the movement words from the poem and use them in sentences of your own.

B. List at least 5 words that describe the different sounds made by a tiger or a lion.

An **oxymoron** is a figure of speech in which two words of opposite meanings are used together.

The most common form of oxymoron involves an **adjective-noun combination**.

Some examples of oxymoron (adjective-noun) are —

open secret	old news
original photocopy	noticeable absence
silent scream	random order

C. Find the oxymoron used in the poem.

Activity

Work in groups of four.

'Animals should be kept in zoos for their own safety.'

Do you agree with this statement?

With the help of a partner, write a debate either for or against the motion.

SUGGESTIONS FOR FURTHER READING

- ***Royal Bengal Tiger***: This poem by Sarwar Chowdhury describes the poet's great admiration for the majestic animal.
- ***Tiger***: This poem by Ernestine Northover gives a detailed description of when and how a tiger stalks and kills its prey.

3

A Lesson for the Teacher

RUSKIN BOND

This is a story about a writer and his servant who shared a deep understanding and had complete faith in each other. Yet something happens that disturbs the writer and shakes his faith in his servant. What happens?

The youth's clothes were second hand and ill-fitting and he had no shoes, but there was self confidence in his **stance** and his smile was sunny.

'Can you give me a job?' he asked.

I hesitated. I was still living alone and I did need someone to help me around the cottage, but I wasn't sure that I could afford the luxury of a servant.

The young man said, 'I've spent all day looking for a suitable person to work for. When I saw you, I decided that no one else had a chance!'

'But can you cook?' I asked.

'I can cook,' he said confidently.

Roop Singh's confidence was not quite matched by his skill.

After taking him on at a **modest wage**, I spent a week instructing him in the mysteries of making omelettes.

stance: A **stance** is the way a person stands.
modest wage: If someone is getting a **modest wage**, he is getting little money for work.

He was a quick learner and was soon serving up some interesting, if not always digestible, meals.

He could light a fire, which was more than a practical writer could achieve, and he had a simple bamboo flute which he played **vigorously** whenever I was at my typewriter.

Roop Singh had done a year or two at school and had started earning a living at the age of twelve. He had worked at various places—tea shops, cycle stands, cinemas, bus stops and railway stations—sometimes as a dishwasher, sometimes as a coolie.

To be a **full-fledged** cook in a bachelor establishment (I doubt if he'd have lasted long in any other kind of establishment!) was a definite advancement, both from the point of view of salary and **prestige**. As soon as he received his first month's pay, he bought himself a pair of shoes, then sent the rest of the money home.

During the afternoons, when he had finished the washing up and I had put my typewriter away, I gave him a few English lessons. 'Teach me something new today,' he would say—a request that I was to hear again and again.

Before long, I had taught Roop Singh to write complete sentences. He looked forward to our sessions under the big deodar tree.

vigorously: If you do something **vigorously**, you do it with great force and energy.
full-fledged: If something is **full-fledged**, it has developed completely to meet certain requirements.
prestige : Prestige is the importance a person gets due to his achievements and success.

I would stretch myself out on a carpet of pine needles, while Roop Singh sat beside me, taking down my dictation in a slow **painstaking** hand. Apart from writing, he loved rolling strange new words around his tongue.

'You are very trusting with your servant,' the local grain merchant warned me one day. 'You should lock up your house when you go out and let the boy sleep elsewhere. Some of these boys turn out to be thieves,' he said.

'But he's been with me a month and I haven't lost anything,' I told him politely.

'Well, don't say I didn't warn you,' he said.

Roop Singh was present when the postman brought me a money order for two hundred rupees, a fee for a story I had written the previous month. It wasn't a very large amount, but it was more than Roop Singh could earn in a month. I put the money in my pocket, and at night, when I went to bed, I placed the **wad** of notes under my pillow. I had never been very careful with my money.

It was a wild stormy night with rain and wind rushing up and down the chimney, rattling[1] the window panes. I slept **fitfully** and was wide awake the moment someone entered the room.

I recognised Roop Singh as he stood outlined against the window, which was frequently lit up by flashes of lightening. He approached my bed, seemed to satisfy himself that I still slept, and then slipped his hand under my pillow.

---

painstaking: If something is done **painstakingly**, it is done with a lot of effort.
wad: A **wad** is a bundle of something.
fitfully: When you sleep **fitfully**, you don't sleep continuously.

I lay perfectly still until he had taken the money, and even then, I did not stir till he had slipped out of the front door. Then, **profoundly** discouraged and too **dismayed** to get up and shut the door, I turned over on my side and lay awake in the dark.

The loss of the money did not trouble me very much, although I knew it would be some time before I sold another story. Undoubtedly, Roop Singh's need was greater than mine, but I felt saddened and lonely and kept telling myself that this would never have happened if I had been a little careful and kept **temptation** out of his way.

I woke to bright sunshine and the shrieking[2] of parrots. Roop Singh was standing beside my bed, a cup of tea in his hands and the usual smile on his face. I sat up on the bed, rubbing my eyes. Had I dreamt the whole thing? Had it all been a horrible **nightmare**?

After Roop Singh had left the room, I put my hand under the pillow and **extracted** the wad of notes.

They were all there, but they were still wet from the night's rain.

So, he had taken the money and he had just as surely brought it back.

> **LITERARY TERM**
> [1] & [2] are examples of **onomatopoeia** or sound words. The sound of the word **rattling** is similar to sound made by the windows and sound of the word **shrieking** is the same as the shrill sound produced by the parrots.

This incident took place some years ago and Roop Singh is still with me. I have never spoken to him about what happened that night or asked him why he came back.

---

profoundly: When you feel **profoundly**, you feel very strongly.
dismayed: If you are **dismayed**, you are disturbed and upset.
temptation: Temptation is a strong attraction towards something that causes somebody to do something wrong.
nightmare: A **nightmare** is a bad dream.
extracted: When you **extract** something, you take it out.

Later, the same day, he came to me with his notebook and pencil, sat down beside me under the Deodar and said, 'Teach me something new today.'

Perhaps that had something to do with it. And I realised that I too had learnt something new.

ABOUT THE AUTHOR

Ruskin Bond (1934-) is an Indian author of British origin. He has written over a hundred short stories, essays, novels and books for children. He is best known for his contribution to children's literature. He received the *Sahitya Academy Award* in 1992 for his book, *Our Trees Still Grow in Dehra*. His stories have been made into films and adapted for TV serials. He lives in Mussourie and loves interacting with children.

Comprehension

A. Arrange the sentences in the order of the events in the story.

1. The writer receives a fee for a story he had written a month ago. ☐
2. That night, Roop Singh quietly steals the money from under the pillow and moves out in the stormy night. ☐
3. The grain merchant warns the writer against trusting his servant blindly. ☐
4. The writer teaches English to Roop Singh and he soon learns to write full sentences. ☐
5. The writer is saddened not by the loss of the money, but by the breach of trust. ☐
6. The writer employs Roop Singh at a modest wage. ☐
7. The writer places the money under his pillow. ☐

8. The writer does not speak about the incident and Roop Singh still works for him. ☐
9. Roop Singh seeks a job with the writer. ☐
10. The next morning, Roop Singh is back and so is the money, though slightly damp. ☐

B. Answer these questions.

1. Why did the writer employ Roop Singh?
2. Explain the line, 'Roop Singh's confidence was not quite matched by his skill.'
3. What impression do you form about Roop Singh's character from the story?
4. Why did the writer trust Roop Singh blindly?
5. Why do you think the writer did not stop Roop Singh from taking the money?
6. Why do you think Roop Singh took the money? Why did he return it?
7. Do you think the writer is a simple man? Give reasons for your answer.
8. What would you have done had you been in the writer's place?
9. 'And I realised that I too had learnt something new.' What did the writer learn?

Vocabulary

A. Given below are a few phrases from the text. Use them to complete the sentences below.

1. sunny smile
2. afford the luxury
3. matched by his/her skill

4. mysteries of cooking
5. a definite advancement
6. a slow painstaking hand
7. slept fitfully
8. lit up by flashes of lightening

1. It was a dark stormy night and the sky was ______________________________
2. The couple earned a small salary and could not ______________________________ of a car.
3. Rohan was promoted to general manager and that was ______________________________ in his career.
4. After the hard labour, Rakesh was exhausted and ______________________________
5. The illiterate woman wrote in a ______________________________
6. Zara soon rose to a top position in the company as her claims were ______________________________
7. When I was old enough to cook, mummy introduced me to the ______________________________
8. Sneha was a cheerful girl and had a ______________________________

B. Given below are a few nouns from the story. Write two suitable adjectives for each of them.

1. hill station ______________ ______________
2. mountainside ______________ ______________
3. sunshine ______________ ______________
4. parrots ______________ ______________
5. cottage ______________ ______________

Activity

Roop Singh had not received any schooling, but he eagerly learnt English from the writer. He knew the value of literacy and education. He put his knowledge to good use by writing a diary entry every day.

Choose any one of the following topics and write a page of Roop Singh's diary. You may write about:

- the day Roop Singh got the job.
- how his master taught him to cook.
- how his master gave him English lessons.
- what he felt when his master received the money order.
- why he stole the money and returned it.

SUGGESTIONS FOR FURTHER READING

- ***Masterji***: This short story by Ruskin Bond is about a chance meeting on the railway platform between a student and his ex-Hindi teacher.
- ***Malgudi Days***: This is a collection of 19 stories written by R. K. Narayan. The stories are all set in the fictional town of Malgudi in South India. Each of the stories describes different events in Malgudi and the people who live there.

4

The Frog Czarina

You may have read the story of the frog that turned into a prince. Here is a story of a princess who was turned into a frog by a wizard. Read the story to find out how she is rescued and gets married to a young Russian prince.

There was once a **czar** who had three sons. When they **came of age**, he **summoned** them. 'My sons,' he said to them, 'I do not know which of you should be selected my successor, so I have decided to pass on the throne to whichever of you makes the best marriage.'

'That's all very well,' the three princes said to themselves, 'but where are we to find ourselves brides so quickly? Let each of us fire an arrow, and wherever it falls, he shall seek his bride.' The eldest son fired his arrow, and it fell at the gate of a certain lord who had a daughter ready for marriage. When the middle son shot his arrow,

czar: A **czar** is an emperor or a king of Russia.
came of age: When a person **comes of age**, he has become an adult.
summoned: To **summon** means to send for someone.

it fell at the door of a rich merchant, who also had a suitable bride among his children. Then, it was the turn of the youngest prince.

The young **czarevich** bent his bow, and his arrow disappeared in the forest. He searched for it and finally found it lying beside a spring. There was a frog sitting on it and it spoke in a human voice, 'Welcome, czarevich. I am your bride!'

So, the young prince arrived home with his bride in a basket. The czar had just sent for his three sons. 'Now, we shall test your brides,' he **proclaimed**. 'Each of them will bake me a loaf of bread by morning!'

When the brides of the two elder sons took their loaves out of the oven, one was hard and burnt, the other soft and sticky. And the frog? At midnight, she leaped out of her basket, changed into a beautiful girl, and clapped her hands. In an instant, there were two bakers standing there. 'What is your wish, **czarina**?' they asked. The frog was none other than an **enchanted** czarina from a neighbouring czardom. An evil magician had cast a spell on her, and human love was the only thing that could set her free.

czarevich: A **czarevich** is the son of a czar.
proclaimed: To **proclaim** is to announce something publicly.
czarina: A **czarina** is an empress of Russia.
enchanted: Someone who is **enchanted** is under a spell.

When morning came, the czarina turned back into a frog. The youngest son took the bread made by the czarina to the czar. It was the finest bread he had ever tasted. Now, he set another task. 'Have each of the brides weave me a carpet before morning!' The moment the brides of the two elder sons began weaving, they got so **entangled** that they could scarcely move. But the youngest prince brought his father a carpet the like of which the czar had never seen before.

Then, the czar ordered his sons to bring their brides to dinner that evening. How amazed the two elder brothers were when the youngest prince led in his beautiful czarina, released from the magician's spell by his love! So, preparations were made for three great weddings.

But the weddings were not to be. The night before they were to take place, the youngest prince found his czarina's frog skin lying in a cupboard, and threw it in the fire. The moment it **went up in smoke**, the czarina disappeared, too. She had fallen back under the spell of the wicked magician. So once more, the young prince set out in search of his bride.

entangled: To get **entangled** is to get caught in something.
went up in smoke: To **go up in a smoke** is to get burned.

A ball of golden thread showed him the way. It rolled into a **thicket** and a huge bear stepped out of it. The prince took up his bow to kill it, but the bear said, 'Spare me, czarevich, and you shall be rewarded!' So he left the bear alone and set off once more to follow the golden thread. Beneath an oak tree, he found a baby eagle that had fallen from its nest. A voice from the tree said, 'Spare my child, and you shall be rewarded!' So, the czarevich let the eaglet go and continued his journey until he came to the bank of a river, where he found a **pike** lying on the ground. 'Put me back in the water, czarevich,' said the fish, 'and you shall be rewarded.' The prince did as he was asked.

Then, he came to the cottage of an old woman. 'I know who you are looking for,' she said. 'Your bride is in the power of an evil magician. To rescue her, you must kill him, and to do that you must release his soul. It is on the point of a needle. The needle is in an egg, the egg is in a duck, and the duck is in an iron box.' She showed him the way.

The prince arrived at the hill on which the magician's castle stood. He had kept the czarina a prisoner there. At the foot of the hill was a tree, and in that tree was the iron box. On a needle, in an egg, in a duck, in that box, was the wizard's soul. Three times the prince tried to climb the tree, and each time he **slid** down again.

He called his friend, the bear. The bear leaned on the tree, and it came tumbling down, and with it, the iron box. Out flew the duck. The czarevich called the eagle and the eagle caught the duck, but the egg fell into the sea. Then he remembered the pike. The fish came in an instant, dived down to the sea bed, and brought the prince the egg. He grabbed hold of it and broke it open, then he took out the needle and broke off its tip. At that moment, the evil magician dropped down dead.

What more is there to tell? A few days later, there was a grand wedding at the czar's palace, as all three of his sons got married. And the youngest of them received his father's czardom as a wedding present.

---

thicket: A **thicket** is a thick growth of bushes.
pike: (here) A **pike** is a kind of freshwater fish.
slid back: To **slide back** is to slip down.

WHAT IS A FAIRY TALE?

The story here is a Russian fairy tale. A fairy tale is a short story involving magical characters and events. It usually features European fantasy characters such as fairies, dwarves, elves, giants and witches. The human characters are usually kings, queens, princes and princesses. The stories typically do not have references to any religion, do not have a moral lesson and have a happy ending, giving birth to the phrase, 'fairy tale ending'.

Comprehension

A. Arrange the sentences in the order of the events in the story.

1. The czar set two tasks for the three brides and the frog czarina won both of them.
2. The czar told his three sons that he would give his czardom to the son who made the best marriage.
3. All the three sons were married and the youngest son was made the successor of the czar.
4. The three princes were to be married, but the frog czarina's frog skin was burnt and she was back under the spell of the wicked magician.
5. The three sons fired an arrow each in the air and found a bride wherever it fell.
6. The third son's arrow fell beside a spring and he took a frog as his bride.
7. The czarina summoned two bakers to bake breads for her.
8. The third son went in search of his bride, led by a ball of golden thread.
9. When the youngest czarevich encountered difficulties in killing the wicked magician, the bear, the eagle and the pike helped him.
10. The prince killed the magician and rescued his bride.

B. Answer these questions.

1. Why did the three princes shoot arrows in the sky?
2. Why did the third prince bring back his bride in a basket?
3. How did the youngest prince prove that he had made the best marriage?
4. 'But the weddings were not to be.' Why did the weddings not take place?
5. Whose lives did the third prince spare while looking for his bride and how was he rewarded?
6. If you were in the place of the youngest prince, would you have married a frog?
7. Write an alternate ending to this story.
8. Suggest another suitable title for the story.

Vocabulary

A. Read the sentences given in the first column. Write down the word which is being described in the meaning.

Sentence	Meaning	Word
The king nominated his eldest daughter as his successor.	*One who is next in line for a title, throne or position*	
He slept beside a spring last night and liked it better than anything else.	*A small stream of water flowing naturally from the earth*	
As a magician, Houdini kept on making his acts increasingly dangerous.	*A person who has the power to make impossible things happen*	

The survivors were rescued by the courageous coast guard.	*To save someone from danger or harm*	
The spell was cast and the man was transformed into a tiger.	*A word or words that have a magical effect*	
I was amazed that they were already familiar with the names of famous designers.	*Suddenly filled with wonder*	
He was sentenced to ten years in prison, but was released after seven years for good behaviour.	*To allow a person/animal to leave a prison or a cage*	
The bomb exploded, and the walls came tumbling down.	*To fall down suddenly and quickly*	

Activity

Imagine you are the enchanted czarina. You are under an evil spell cast by a wicked wizard and have been transformed into a frog. Think of the events that take place in your life after that and how you feel about them.

Express your feelings on being changed into a frog.

SUGGESTIONS FOR FURTHER READING

- ***The Frog King or Iron Heinrich***: This is a story by Jacob and Wilhelm Grimm about a handsome prince who had been enchanted by a witch and turned into a frog.
- ***Beauty and the Beast***: This is a fairy tale written by French novelist Jeanne-Marie Leprince de Beaumont. The story recounts the tale of a prince turned into a hideous beast by the curse of a fairy.

5

Packing for the Trip

JEROME K. JEROME

Do you enjoy packing for trips?
Read the story of three friends, J, George and Harris, who decide to take a boat trip down the River Thames. As they try to pack for the trip, it turns out to be a funny process. Read on to find out how they go about it.

We made a list of the things to be taken. The next day, we got them all together, and met in the evening to pack. I said I'd pack. I rather pride myself on my packing. I told George and Harris that they had better leave the whole matter entirely to me.

They fell into the suggestion readily. George spread himself over the easy chair, and Harris put his legs on the table. This was hardly what I intended. What I had meant, of course, was that I should boss the job, and that Harris and George should **potter** about under my directions.

Their taking it in the way they did irritated me.

However, I did not say anything, but started the packing. It seemed a longer job than I had thought it was going to be, but I got the bag finished at last.

'Ain't you going to put the boots in?' said Harris.

---

potter: When you **potter**, you move unhurriedly and aimlessly.

And I looked round and found I had forgotten them. That's just like Harris. He couldn't have said a word until I'd got the bag shut. And George laughed one of those irritating, senseless laughs of his. They do make me so wild.

I opened the bag and packed the boots in, and then, just as I was going to close it, a horrible idea occurred to me. Had I packed my toothbrush?

My toothbrush is a thing that haunts me when I'm travelling, and makes my life a misery. Of course, I had to turn every **mortal** thing out now, and of course, I could not find it.

Of course, I found George's and Harris's eighteen times over, but I couldn't find my own. Then, I found it inside a boot. I repacked once more.

The bag got shut up finally at 10.05 p.m. and then there remained the **hampers** to do.

Harris said that we should be wanting to start in less than twelve hours' time, and thought that he and George had better do the rest, and I agreed and they had a go.

They began in a light-hearted **spirit**. I made no comment, I only waited.

When George is hanged, Harris will be the worst packer in this world, and I looked at the piles of plates and cups, and kettles, and bottles and jars, and pies, and stoves, and cakes, and tomatoes and felt that the thing would soon become exciting.

It did. They started by breaking a cup. Then, Harris packed the strawberry jam on top of a tomato and **squashed** it, and they had to pick out the tomato with a teaspoon.

mortal: Everything that dies or is destroyed after sometime is **mortal**.

hampers: (here) A **hamper** is a basket with a handle and a lid, used for carrying food, cutlery, and plates on a picnic.

spirit: (here) **Spirit** is a special attitude or frame of mind

squashed: If something is **squashed**, it is pressed in a manner that it loses its shape.

And then, it was George's turn, and he **trod** on the butter. I didn't say anything, but I came over and sat on the edge of the table and watched them. It irritated them more than anything I could have said. They packed the pies at the bottom, and put heavy things on top, and flattened the pies.

They upset salt over everything, and as for the butter, I never saw two men do more with one-and-two pence worth of butter in my whole life than they did! After George had got it off his slipper, they tried to put it in the kettle. It wouldn't go in, and what WAS in wouldn't come out.

They did **scrape** it out at last, and put it down on a chair, and Harris sat on it, and it stuck to him, and they went looking for it all over the room.

'I'll take my oath I had put it down on that chair,' said George, staring at the empty seat.

'I saw you do it myself,' said Harris.

Then, they started round the room again, looking for it, and then they met again in the centre and stared at one another.

'Most extraordinary thing I ever heard of,' said George. 'So mysterious!' said Harris.

Then, George got round at the back of Harris and saw it.

trod: If you **tread** on something, you step on it.

scrape: If you **scrape** something, you use a hard and sharp instrument to remove something from where it is stuck.

'Why, here it is all the time,' he exclaimed **indignantly**. 'Where?' cried Harris, **spinning** round.

'Stand still, can't you!' roared George, flying after him.

And they got it off, and packed it in the teapot.

Montmorency, our pet, was in it all, of course.

He came and sat down on things just when they were wanted to be packed, and he laboured under the fixed belief that whenever Harris or George reached out their hand for anything, it was his cold, damp nose that they wanted.

He put his leg into the jam, and he pretended that the lemons were rats, and got into the hamper and killed three of them before Harris could **land** him with the frying-pan.

The packing was done at 12.50 a.m. Harris sat on the big hamper and said he hoped nothing would be found broken. George said that if anything was broken it was broken, which, on **reflection**, seemed to comfort him. He also said he was ready for bed.

We were all ready for bed.

ABOUT THE AUTHOR

Jerome Klapka Jerome (1859 – 1927) was an English author, best known for the humorous novel, *Three Men in a Boat*. Though this novel is not autobiographical, the three main characters are his friends and Jerome himself. The book has been made into a movie and television series. He has written other novels, short stories, essays, plays and an autobiography. He was the editor of a magazine, *The Idler*, for a short while.

indignantly: If someone speaks **indignantly**, he speaks in an angry manner.
spinning: Something that is **spinning** is turning quickly.
land: (here) To **land** someone is to hit him/her to stop his/her activities.
reflection: A **reflection** is a thought or an idea.

Comprehension

A. Choose the correct answer.

1. The author is annoyed with his friends when he decides to pack because
   a. they did not allow him to pack.
   b. they did not help him in packing.
   c. they said he did not know how to pack.
2. The author's toothbrush is a thing that haunts him when he travels because
   a. he always forgets to pack it.
   b. he is never sure that he has packed it.
   c. it always gets lost in the journey.
3. George and Harris were irritated with J because
   a. he offered to help them with packing.
   b. he made fun of their packing.
   c. he just sat and watched them making mistakes in packing.
4. George and Harris could not find the butter because
   a. it was packed under the pies.
   b. Harris had sat on it and it was stuck to his back.
   c. Montmorency, their pet, had eaten it.

B. Answer these questions.

1. J told George and Harris that they had better leave the whole packing entirely to him. What did he really mean when he said this?
2. Why did J have to reopen the bag after he had just finished packing it?

3. Why did he open it a third time?
4. What was J's opinion about George and Harris' skill at packing?
5. Mention three things George and Harris did to prove J's opinion about them was right.
6. How was the butter packed?
7. What was Montmorency's contribution to the packing?
8. 'We were all ready for bed.' Why does the author make this statement?
9. Which incident in the story did you find the most hilarious? Give reasons for your answer.
10. What do you think about the packing skill of the three friends?

Vocabulary

A. Write if these sentences are true (T) or false(F).

1. If you **irritate** someone, you make them happy.
2. If you **boss** someone, you make that person work under your supervision.
3. If you **spread yourself** over a chair, you make yourself uncomfortable.
4. To **haunt** someone is to follow and bother someone.
5. To be **light-hearted** is to have a small heart.
6. If you **smash** something, you crush it to pieces.

B. Match the phrases with their meanings.

Phrases	Meanings
1. pride oneself	a. to obey orders
2. fall into suggestion	b. to run after someone
3. under one's directions	c. to agree easily
4. make one wild	d. to try
5. have a go	e. be proud of
6. fly after someone	f. to make someone very angry

Activity

A. Work in groups of four. Pick any part of the story and enact it.

B. Create a short cartoon strip with dialogues, showing how the packing was done. Choose one of the following situations:

- how the author packed and repacked the suitcase
- how George and Harris packed the butter
- the contributions made by Montmorency to the packing

SUGGESTIONS FOR FURTHER READING

- ***The Worst Class Trip Ever***: This story by Dave Barry is about an eighth-grader, Wyatt Palmer, his best friend, Matt, and a few kids from Culver Middle School who go on a class trip to Washington, DC, with their teachers. The story describes their attempts to stay out of trouble with their teachers and their adventures while trying to save the President!
- ***Chitty Chitty Bang Bang***: This is a novel written by Ian Fleming for his son, Caspar. It is a tale about a professor who invents a magical flying car called Chitty Chitty Bang Bang. The delightful adventures of the car and the Pott family are narrated in the story.

6

November

ALICE CARY

Autumn is also called the fall because the trees shed their leaves in autumn. Will this autumn stay forever? Read this poem to find out.

The leaves are fading and falling,[1]
The winds are rough and wild,
The birds have **ceased** their calling,
But let me tell you, my child.
Though day by day, as it closes,
Doth darker and colder grow,
The roots of the bright red roses
Will keep alive in the snow.

And when the Winter is over,
The **boughs** will get new leaves,
The **quail** come back to the **clover**,
And the swallow back to the **eaves**.
The leaves to-day are **whirling**,
The brooks are dry and dumb,[2]
But let me tell you, my darling,
The Spring will be sure to come.

ceased: Ceased means stopped.
doth: Doth is the old English word for 'does'.
bough: A **bough** is the main branch of a tree.
quail: A **quail** is a small wild bird.
clover: A **clover** is a small plant that has three leaves on each stem.
eaves: Eaves is the lower edge of a roof that overhangs the wall.
whirling: When something **whirls**, it moves round and round rapidly.

So, when some dear joy loses
Its **beauteous** summer flow,
Think how the roots of the roses
Are kept alive in the snow.

LITERARY TERM

1 & 2 are examples of **alliteration**. 'Fading and falling' begin with the same consonant sound, 'f' and 'dry and dumb' begin with the same consonant sound, 'd'.

beauteous: Something that is **beauteous** is beautiful.

Comprehension

A. Read the following lines and answer the questions that follow.

1. *Though day by day, as it closes,*
   Doth darker and colder grow,
   The roots of the bright red roses
   Will keep alive in the snow.
   a. Which season is the poet referring to?
   b. Why does the poet use the phrase, 'bright red roses'?
   c. How are the roots of the roses kept alive?
2. *The leaves to-day are whirling,*
   The brooks are dry and dumb,
   a. Which season is the poet referring to here?
   b. Why are the leaves 'whirling'?
   c. Why does the poet say that the brooks are 'dumb'?
3. *So, when some dear joy loses*
   Its beauteous summer flow,
   Think how the roots of the roses
   Are kept alive in the snow.
   a. Explain the first two lines of the extract.
   b. What have roses been compared to in these lines?
   c. What does snow symbolise in these lines?

B. Answer these questions briefly.

1. Explain the meaning of the line, 'The Spring will be sure to come.'
2. What will happen to the trees when winter is over?

C. Answer these questions.

1. How does the poet indicate the season the poem is set in? Give examples from the poem to support your answer.
2. How does the poet indicate the onset of spring?
3. In the sixth stanza, is the poet talking only about winter? Give reasons for your answer.
4. Has November been compared to difficult times in life? Support your answer with examples from the poem.
5. What is the message of the poem.
6. Think of another suitable title for the poem.
7. The poet has described two seasons here. Complete the following organiser to show the contrast between the two seasons.

Autumn		Spring
falling, fading	Leaves	new leaves
	Birds	
	Winds	
	Temperature	

The language of poetry

Alliteration is a literary device where a series of closely placed words have the same first consonant sound. For example, fading and falling

Have you noticed that a few popular companies, such as Dunkin Donuts, use alliteration in their brand names?

A. Write names of five more companies that use this literary technique to make the name of their company catchy and easy to remember.

B. Write down all the rhyming words of the poem.

C. Write two rhyming words each for the following words:

bird bough root rose

Activity

Work in groups of six. Create a PowerPoint presentation (about 10-12 slides) on the poem.

Type the stanzas of the poem and use pictures from the Internet to illustrate the poem. For example,

- leafless trees covered with snow
- bright red roses
- a quail
- swallow's nest under the eaves

SUGGESTIONS FOR FURTHER READING

- ***Autumn***: This is a poem by Alice Cary that gives a vibrant and colourful description of nature during the autumn season.
- ***Life***: This poem by Sarojini Naidu describes life as being full of difficulties.

7

A Quick-witted Person

A trickster is a person who deceives or cheats people and harms them. But sometimes, these tricksters even get rewarded. Read this folk tale to know how a trickster was rewarded.

There was once a **destitute** man called Tong who one day happened to meet another young man, also named Tong. Having chatted with one another, Big Tong and Small Tong decided to become friends and help each other earn a living.

Small Tong suggested that Big Tong become a **monk**. Big Tong hesitated at first, but later agreed when Small Tong insisted that his monkhood would only be a means of living. Having found a **deserted** temple, Big Tong had his head shaved, **donned** a yellow robe, and led the life of a **bogus** monk there.

Small Tong, meanwhile, went about from village to village, stealing cattle from the villagers, hiding them in deep forests and reporting back to the **venerable** Tong about what he had done. Small Tong told the

destitute: A **destitute** is a person who is very poor.
monk: A **monk** is a member of a religious group who vows to stay poor and unmarried.
deserted: A **deserted** place is one where no one lives.
donned: To **don** is to wear.
bogus: Something that is **bogus** is false.
venerable: A **venerable** person is someone who is respected highly because of his age and wisdom.

villagers that there was a monk who was a true **crystal ball gazer** and could tell them where to look for the lost cattle.

The villagers, **disheartened** at having lost their cattle, went to ask the venerable Tong where to find them.

The venerable Tong, pretending to draw a few lines on a slate, told each villager where to find his cattle. The villagers would, then, go into the forest and find the cattle as foretold by the monk.

They were very pleased and as a token of gratitude, they showered the monk with all kinds of gifts.

One day, the governor of the land lost his diamond ring. He sent his aide to ask the venerable Tong to locate it. When the **aide** told him what had happened, Tong was **panic-stricken**, thinking he would soon be in trouble, and cursed himself, 'Your day has come, Tong. No one can help you now.'

Now, the name of the aide who came to ask Tong to find the governor's diamond ring was also Tong. When he heard the venerable Tong's curses, he was frightened and turned very pale. He cried and confessed that he was the one who had stolen the governor's diamond ring. To **redeem** himself, he told the venerable Tong where to find the ring and asked him to help save his life. The venerable Tong was pleased that luck had come his way again.

He hurried to the governor and told him where to find the ring, but refused to identify the culprit, saying that as a monk he had to be kind. The governor raised no objection.

---

crystal ball gazer: A **crystal ball gazer** tells the future by looking into a crystal ball.
disheartened: If you are **disheartened**, you have lost all hope.
aide: An **aide** is someone who acts as an assistant to an officer.
panic-stricken: If you are **panic-stricken**, you are too frightened to think or act logically.
redeem: To **redeem** is to make up for the wrong that is done.

When the ring was found, the monk was rewarded with valuable gifts and a **sumptuous** meal. The venerable Tong was so pleased that he **gobbled** down the food very fast.

As a result, a chicken bone got stuck in his throat. He felt embarrassed to bring it out, as the governor was present there.

All he could do was to move his head up and down. The governor thought he was asking him to come closer. No sooner had he moved to approach the venerable Tong than thunder struck the pillar against which he had been leaning.

The thunder frightened the venerable Tong so much that he swallowed the chicken bone and fell unconscious.

When he regained consciousness, he told the governor that he had a **premonition** that thunder was going to strike the pillar. That is why he signalled to him to move away from there. The governor was so pleased that he invited the venerable Tong to stay at the royal temple.

One day, a cobra got into the pond in the palace grounds.

No one dared to use water from that pond. The governor asked for Tong's help. Being frightened himself, Tong peeped into the pond to see how big the cobra was.

---

sumptuous meal: A **sumptuous meal** is very delicious and expensive.
gobble: To **gobble** is to eat very quickly and in large mouthfuls.
premonition: A **premonition** is a feeling that something bad is going to happen.

Unfortunately, he slipped and fell into the water. In panic, he grasped whatever was at hand. When he regained composure, he realised that he was holding the cobra's neck.

Stories of Tong's heroic deed spread far and wide. Soon after this, enemies **besieged** the town. The governor asked Tong to lead the army in **combat**. Tong did not know how to ride a horse. To prevent him from falling off of the horse, Small Tong tied the venerable Tong's feet together under the horse's stomach.

When the horse started to gallop, the venerable Tong lost control and slipped from its back, **dangling** under the seat. His two feet which were tied together, were seen pointing upwards.

The enemies had never seen anyone riding a horse in that position. The enemy soldiers thought that the venerable Tong was using black magic to kill them. They ran **helter-skelter**. Victory then belonged to the venerable Tong.

After being helped to sit upright on the horse, he explained that by hanging his head down, he was trying to avoid the enemies' black magic and, at the same time, was using his own black magic to drive them away.

This victory won the venerable Tong a great deal of fame.

---

beseige: If you **beseige** a town, you surround it with soldiers and try to take control of it.
combat: A **combat** is a battle.
dangling: Something that is **dangling** is hanging loosely.
helter-skelter: When you run **helter-skelter**, you run in a disorderly manner.

Comprehension

A. Fill in the boxes to create a flowchart of the story.

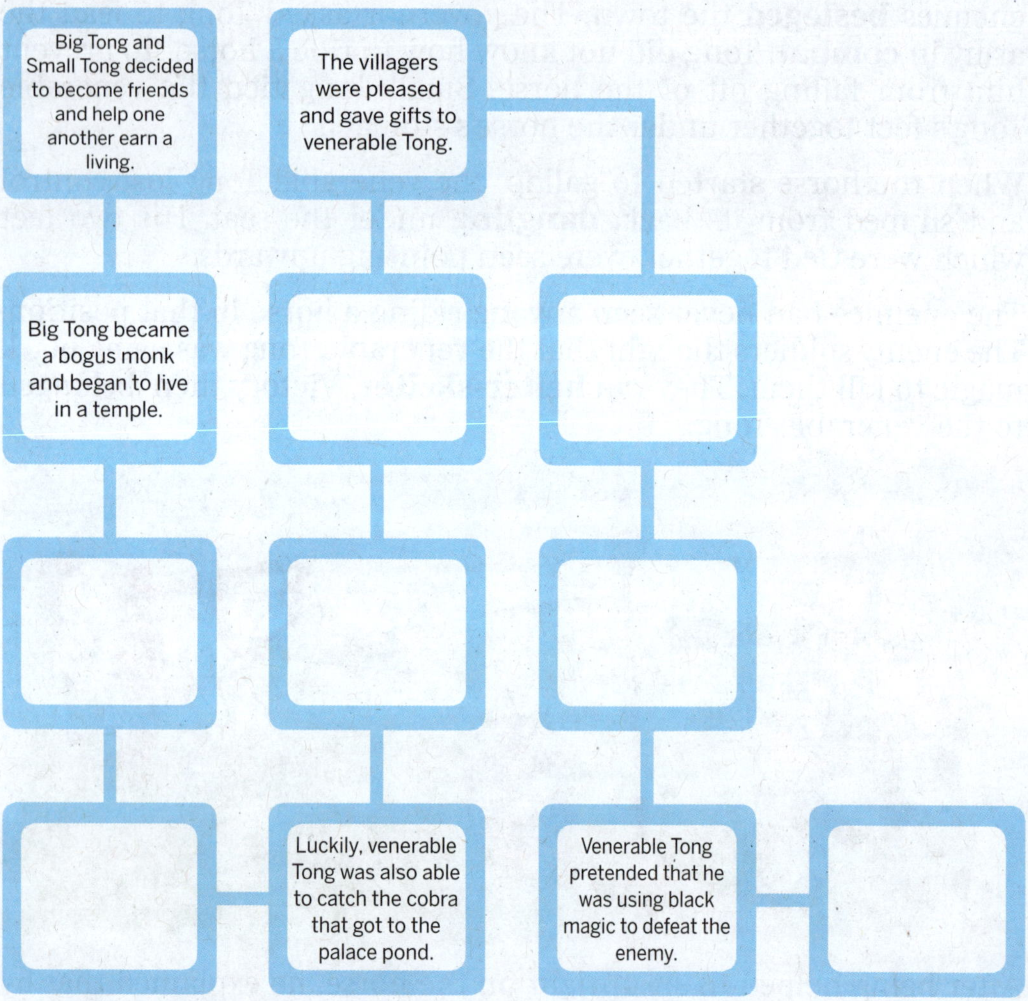

B. Answer these questions.

1. Why did venerable Tong become a monk? Was he a real monk?
2. How did the Small Tong and venerable Tong trick the villagers and earn money?

3. How was the venerable Tong able to find the governor's lost diamond ring? Did he deserve credit for finding it?
4. Narrate the second incident through which the venerable Tong earned the governor's gratitude.
5. The venerable Tong won praise when the attacking enemy ran helter-skelter. Do you think he deserved the recognition? Why/Why not?
6. Some people would say that Small Tong and the venerable Tong were quick-witted and very lucky. What is your opinion?
7. What do you think happened to Small Tong and the venerable Tong after the war was won?

Vocabulary

A. These words from the story have been used to describe people and their actions. Use them to complete the sentences below.

frightened unconscious embarrassed bogus heroic pleased kind

1. The ____________________ fireman entered the burning building and saved many lives.
2. When Harry wove a long story as an excuse for coming late, the teacher immediately realised that the story was ____________________
3. The electric eel suddenly swam out from behind the rocks and the deep sea divers were ____________________
4. The bully threw the little boy into the deep end of the pool as a prank. The boy did not know swimming and when he was finally rescued, he was ____________________

5. Joyesh was the only one who did not know his dialogues. He was really ________________ when it was his turn on the stage.
6. The beggar was touched by the generosity of the ________________ stranger.
7. The board results have been declared today and I am very ________________ as I have secured first rank.

Activity

The venerable Tong got into many difficult situations but managed to come out of them with ease because he was lucky and clever.

- Think of another complex situation in which the venerable Tong finds himself but uses it to his advantage.
- Write about the incident. Share your story with your classmates.
- Decide amongst the class who has written the funniest and cleverest incident.

SUGGESTIONS FOR FURTHER READING

- ***Fascinating Folktales of Thailand***: This is a book that contains ancient stories of Thailand so that people of other countries can understand and appreciate the culture and values of traditional Thailand.
- ***The Trickster Tricked***: This is a Native American legend retold by S. E. Schlosser. It is a story about a turtle that defeats a rabbit in the race not because the rabbit fell asleep but by playing a trick on the rabbit, with the help of his family.

8

From a Railway Carriage

ROBERT LOUIS STEVENSON

In the 19th century, when this poem was written, the speed of a steam engine appeared magical to the travellers. It was faster than anything they had seen before. Read this poem and find out how travellers felt and what they saw as they sat in a steam engine train.

Faster than fairies, faster
than witches,
Bridges and houses, hedges
and **ditches**;
And charging along like
troops in a battle[1]
All through the meadows
the horses and cattle:
All of the sights of the hill
and the plain
Fly as thick as **driving
rain**;[2]
And ever again, **in the
wink of an eye**,
Painted stations whistle by.

ditches: A **ditch** is a long narrow hole that is dug along a road or field,
troop: A **troop** is a group of soldiers.
driving rain: Driving rain is an expression used to refer to rain that is falling with great force and speed.
in the wink of an eye: If something happens **in the wink of an eye**, it happens very quickly.

Here is a child who **clambers** and **scrambles**,
All by himself and gathering **brambles**;
Here is a tramp who stands and gazes;
And here is the green for stringing the daisies!

Here is a cart runaway in the road
Lumping along with man and load;
And here is a mill, and there is a river:
Each a glimpse and gone forever!

LITERARY TERM

❶ & ❷ are examples of **similes**. In ❶, the poet has compared the fast movement of the train to that of soldiers in a battle. In ❷, the sights seen from the train window seem to fly by like heavy rainfall and appear to be blurry.

clambers: When a person **clambers**, he climbs in an awkward fashion.
scrambles: To **scramble** is to move or climb over something quickly, using your hands.
brambles: Brambles are rough bushes or vines that have sharp thorns on their branches.
lumping: Lumping is moving slowly, heavily and awkwardly.

ABOUT THE POET

Robert Louis Stevenson (1850 - 1894) was a Scottish novelist, poet, essayist, and travel writer. His most famous works are *Treasure Island, Kidnapped*, and *The Strange Case of Dr Jekyll and Mr Hyde*. He also wrote many beautiful poems.

Comprehension

A. Complete the sentences by choosing the correct option.

1. The poem is mainly about
   a. the invention of the steam engine.
   b. dangers of travelling by train.
   c. the people and places seen from a fast moving train.
2. The train is moving faster than
   a. fairies and witches.
   b. troops in the battle.
   c. horses and cattle.

3. The line 'Each a glimpse and gone forever!' means

   a. the train is moving slowly and you can take a good look at things but you won't see them again.

   b. the train is moving fast but you can see things clearly.

   c. the train is moving fast, you can take a quick look at things, but you won't see them again.

B. Answer the questions.

1. Why do you think the poet has written this poem?
2. The poem was written in the nineteenth century, before fast cars and aeroplanes were invented. So train travel would have seemed very fast and exciting. How does the poet make it magical as well?
3. Which is the only other mode of transport mentioned in the poem? What effect does the poet create by mentioning it?
4. What does the poet mean when he says, 'painted stations whistle by'?
5. Who were the three people that were seen from the window of the moving train?
6. What kind of terrain is the train moving through?
7. Is the train moving very fast? Give examples from the poem to support your answer.
8. When you read the poem, what does the rhythm of the poem remind you of?
9. How do you think the poet feels after this train journey?

The language of poetry

A. The poet has used a few words to denote sound in the poem. For example, whistle

Make a list of the words that express sound in the poem.

B. The poet has used several words to denote the movement of the train.

Put these words in order from slowest to fastest.

charging along	fly	driving	in a wink
whistle by	clambers	scrambles	run away
lumping along	stands		

C. Similes are a way of describing something by comparing it with something else.

Create your own similies.

as heavy as ____________________

as fast as ____________________

as slow as ____________________

as clean as ____________________

as lazy as ____________________

Activity

The poet has described what can be seen outside the train. But a lot also happens inside a train too.

A. Think of a train journey you have taken. Then, along with your partner, write a detailed description of what can be heard, seen and even smelt inside a railway coach.

You may write about the following:

- the people sitting inside the train
- the luggage stacked inside the train
- the conversation of the passengers
- the vendors and their calls
- the smell of the food being served
- the playful/weepy children

B. Read this short and descriptive poem that uses a lot of onomatopoeic words to create a clear image of the journey of a freight train. Learn it and recite it in class.

The Freight Train

Clickity, clackity, clickity clack!
The train speeds over the railroad track.
It rolls and rattles and screeches its song
And pulls and jiggles its freight cars along.
Clickity, clackity, clickity, clack!
The engine in front is big and black.
The cars are filled with lots of things
Like milk, or oil, or mattress spings.
Clickity, clackity, clickity, clack!
The engineer waves, and I wave back.
I count the cars as the freight train goes
and the whistle blows and blows ... and blows!

Now, make a list of the onomatopoeic words used in the poem.

SUGGESTIONS FOR FURTHER READING

- ***The Night Mail***: Written by W. H. Auden, this is a simple poem highlighting the tireless and unceasing work done by the efficient staff of a night mail train. It also describes various fields, meadows, and how the train rushes to reach its destination on time.

9

Sam Spook's Triumph - I

M. S. MAHADEVAN

Do ghosts like human beings? How do they feel when they see human beings? Discuss with your friends. Then, read this humorous story to find out if you are right.

'Mummy...' Sam Spook shrieked. 'Quick ... help!'

'What is it, Sam?' his mother asked. 'Did you have a bad dream?'

Sam looked at her wordlessly. He was shaking all over. He pointed a **trembling** finger at the wardrobe. 'There is a human in there. A live one.'

'Oh no, Sam. Not again!' his mother sighed. 'Can't you see I am dressed to go out?

'He is there,' Sam insisted. 'A horrible, flesh and blood human. If you leave me alone, he will come again to frighten me.' 'You are being silly,' said his mother.

She went to the wardrobe and flung open the door for her son.

'Look, there is no one in here. Now, are you satisfied?'

'Maybe he is under the bed,' Sam said.

trembling: When someone is **trembling**, that person is shaking slightly because of fear or cold.

His mother looked under the bed. She checked behind the curtains and under the bookshelf.

The next night, it happened again. 'Mummy ... help! Come quickly.'

'Go to sleep, Sam,' his mother called out sleepily.

A few minutes later, she was disturbed by the **patter**[1] of little feet. 'Can I get into your **sarcophagus**?' Sam pleaded, 'There is a horrible live human in my room. With bad breath!'

'It is just a nightmare. Sam ... oh, all right. Get in.'

Tucked between his parents, Sam felt safe.

'This has got to stop,' Sam's father said the next morning.

'Yes dear, but you know how it is. He is just a baby, only hundred and ten years old. He will grow out of it.'

'Anyway, I think I will have a word with him.'

Sam's father found him feeding his pet bat. He picked Sam up and carried him piggyback into the garden. Making him sit down, he began, 'Son, tell me what the problem is. Why are you scared of live humans?'

'They are loud and **clumsy**,' Sam said. 'They keep bumping into things instead of going right through them, like us.'

'That is because they have bodies, son.'

'What does anyone need a body for? It is such a bother. It blocks the view. It needs regular feeding and cleaning. Humans eat thrice a day. Imagine that!'

---

patter: A **patter** is a quick succession of light sounds.
sarcophagus: A **sarcophagus** is a stone coffin.
clumsy: If you are **clumsy**, you are unable to do things gracefully.

Sam's father smiled. 'They need to keep body and soul together, son.' Sam **shuddered**.

'Every ghost was once a human. It is just that we have moved on. Now, what I want you to remember is that it takes all kinds to make the world. And don't be scared of humans.'

'I will try, Dad,' Sam promised.

'Well, I must be off to work.' Sam's father got up and put on his coat. He ran a famous acting school for spirits.

'I think I will walk today,' he said. 'I need the exercise. I have a feeling that I have put on a few grams. If I don't watch out, I will become human all over again.'

'That is not funny, Dad!' Sam protested.

On his way out, Sam's father stopped by the kitchen where his wife was tidying up and said, 'By the way, I have two of our visiting professors over for dinner.'

'Oh, dear!' Sam's mother sighed.[2]

'As usual, you picked a busy day. Anyway, I will do the shopping on my way back. Tell me, whom have you invited?'

'The banshee of Kilkenny Castle, Ireland and Haroun the djinn, from Turkey. See you later.'

LITERARY TERMS

[1] & [2] are examples of **onomatopoeia**. The pronunciation of the words 'patter' and 'sighed' is the same as the sound they represent.

---

shuddered: When you **shudder**, you tremble with fear.

For the rest of the morning, Sam's mother rushed through her household **chores**, got him dressed and dropped him at Aunt Churail's playschool. She arranged with the Doppelgänger twins' mother to drop Sam home.

'I might be a bit late getting back,' she said. 'Don't get up to any mischief, Sam.'

'Can I play with the skeleton in the cupboard till you get back?'

'Yes, but don't be rough with him. He is ten thousand years old.' Sam promised to be as good as a ghoul.

He spent the rest of the morning playing Hide and Spook with the Doppelgänger twins, Dolly Demon and Chotu-Motu, the noisy Poltergeist brothers. Later, Aunt Churail taught them a new nursery rhyme, 'The Ghoul and the Pussy Cat'. During the storytelling hour, she told them a new tale about Vikram and Betaal and on popular demand, 'Spook in Boots'.

Then, it was time to go home.

'You sure, you will be okay?' the Doppelgänger twins' mother asked Sam, after he had got off the broomstick.

'I will be fine,' Sam said confidently.

---

chore: A **chore** is an everyday task around the house.

Comprehension

A. Match the following phrases to make sentences.

Column A	Column B
1. Sam Spook was afraid	a. of Sam's imaginary fears.
2. His mother was tired	b. of human beings.
3. Sam's father ran a	c. as they were loud and clumsy.
4. Sam Spook was scared of humans	d. playschool when she had to go to work.
5. His mother dropped Sam at Aunt Churail's	e. famous acting school for spirits.

B. Answer these questions.

1. How old was Sam Spook? Why did his mother call him a 'baby'?
2. Why has the author shown that 'baby' ghosts are afraid of human beings?
3. How was Sam Spook like an ordinary human child?
4. How has the author shown that Sam's father was like human fathers?
5. Compare Sam's mother's activities with your mother's activities. Are they same or different?

6. What if you were Sam Spook? Would you behave in the same way as he did? What would you do?
7. Are you afraid of ghosts? What do you do when you imagine there is a ghost in your room?

Vocabulary

The chapter contains many words connected with ghosts.

A. Use your dictionary to find the meanings of these words and write a brief description of each.

1. sarcophagus
2. banshee
3. djinn
4. doppelgänger
5. churail
6. poltergeist
7. ghoul

B. Circle the best verb to complete the sentences.

1. My fingers were trembling/moving as I picked up my guitar to play in front of the large audience.
2. His sleep was woken/disturbed by the sound of trucks on the street.
3. Vipul was eating/feeding scraps of meat to his pet dog.
4. Mrs Potter ran/walked a school for young wizards.
5. You compromised/promised that you wouldn't go into the woods alone.

Activity

Imagine you are Sam Spook's friend. Sam has written a letter to you about how he is afraid of human beings. He feels ashamed that despite his age, he should be scared in this way. He wants to be rid of such fears.

In response to his letter, write a letter of advice to him on what he should do to be free from such fears.

SUGGESTIONS FOR FURTHER READING

- ***Vetal Pachisi***: Originally written in Sanskrit, this is a collection of 25 tales about the attempts made by the legendary King Vikramaditya to capture a ghost.
- ***A Christmas Carol***: This novel by Charles Dickens describes how the miser, Ebenezer Scrooge, is changed into a kind and generous person by four ghosts that visit him.

10

Sam Spook's Triumph - II

M. S. MAHADEVAN

After being troubled by imaginary fears, Sam finally comes in contact with real, live humans. What is his reaction? Who is more frightened- Sam or the humans? Who chases whom away? Read on to find out.

Sam ran through the rusty iron gates of the old ***haveli*** that was his home. He **glided** up the overgrown drive, past the ruined summerhouse, right through the big wooden door and up the sweeping staircase.

The house was quiet just as he liked it.

Cro-Magnon Man, the skeleton in the cupboard, was Sam's favourite toy. His father had picked it up on his last visit to France. The Cro-Magnon Man was a life-size, battery-operated walkie-talkie. It made deep sounds and walked in stiff, jerky movements.

Sam **wound** up the Cro-Magnon Man.

haveli: ***Haveli*** is the Hindi word for a large, impressive house.
glided: When something glides, it moves smoothly.
wound: (here) To **wind** something means to tighten its springs to make it work.

The toy walked a few steps and came to an **abrupt** stop. The battery was running down. Or probably there was a loose connection. Sam was about to **investigate** when there was a disturbance.

'Just look at the size of this place,' a voice boomed.[1]

A human voice! Sam froze. It could not be! Live humans. And they were in his house!

'Ugh ... these **ghastly** cobwebs!' a female voice said.

Sam shook with rage. Ghastly cobwebs! His mother was proud of those cobwebs. They were designer cobwebs. She had paid a small fortune for them.

Then, he heard something that sent a shock-wave through him. 'Don't worry about the cobwebs. They will be pulled down along with the rest of this ruin.' It was a man's voice. 'In its place, we will have a smart holiday resort with a pool, a disco, tennis courts, restaurants, casinos, a band, crowds of happy people, and money flowing into our **coffers**. Get the picture?'

The two humans laughed.

Sam was **petrified**. If he had ears, he would not have believed them. Pull down this ruin! Why, this was one of the most beautiful, stately ruins in the country. Touring

abrupt: Something that is **abrupt** is sudden or unexpected.
investigate: When you **investigate** something, you try to find out all the facts about it.
ghastly: Something that is **ghastly** is horrible and frightening.
coffer: A **coffer** is a box, usually for storing money.
petrified: When someone is **petrified**, he is terribly frightened.

spirits from other lands came to admire it. And these humans were planning to **demolish** it!

Sam knew what that meant. There would be bulldozers and men with shovels. There would be trucks and concrete mixers. And what would happen to him and his family? They would join the increasing number of **displaced** spirits. Where would they go? What would they do? Maybe they would have no other choice but to move to a city. Imagine having to haunt a huge apartment complex. For a ghost, it was death.

He had to do something to stop it. But what could he do? He was so small. And he was terrified.

Use reason, his father would tell Sam. With reason, you can overcome fear. It is, also, a far better way of making your point than using muscle. Anyway, ghosts do not have muscles, he had added with a quiet **chuckle**.

Maybe he can reason with them, Sam thought. Maybe if he explained what this house meant to them, they might understand. It was worth a try.

The footsteps stopped right outside the door. Sam **steeled himself** for his first sight of humans. The door **creaked**[2] open. Despite his brave intentions, Sam was petrified. The humans were in the room. He could hear them, smell them ...

Suddenly, there was a low growl.

The Cro-Magnon Man moved. He took a few unsteady steps towards the intruders.

The woman **shrieked**.[3] A long, loud scream that would have surely aroused the envy of the visiting banshee of Kilkenny Castle! It seemed to go on and on. It was the man's face that really got Sam's attention. The huge

LITERARY TERMS

1, 2 & 3 are examples of **onomatopoeia**. 'Boom' sounds like the noise made by a deep voice. 'Creaked' sounds like the sound made by an old door and 'shrieked' sounds like the sharp shrill sound produced by a frightened person.

demolish: When you **demolish** something, you destroy it.
displaced: A **displaced** person is one who has no home.
chuckle: A **chuckle** is a quiet laugh.
steeled himself: When someone **steels himself**, he gathers up his courage to do something.

flesh and blood man had turned as pale as a ghost! [4] His eyes **bulged**. His mouth opened and shut, mechanically, **mimicking** the Cro-Magnon Man's jaw movement. For a long time, no sound emerged.

But when it did '... AAARRRGGGHHH ...' It even stopped the Cro-Magnon Man in his tracks.

The humans turned around and still screaming loud enough to wake the dead, **took to their heels**.

Long after they had gone, their screams echoed through the ruined haveli.

Now, what was that all about, Sam wondered as he repaired the loose wire in the toy.

For a moment, it had seemed as if the two humans were scared, actually scared of the Cro-Magnon Man. But that was impossible.

How could anyone be scared of a mere skeleton?

Yet, he had a feeling that they were not coming back in a hurry.

It was a rather nice feeling.

LITERARY TERMS

[4] This is an example of a **simile**. The colour of the man's face has been compared to the colour of a ghost, using the word 'as'.

---

bulged: Something that **bulges** swells in an unnatural way.
mimicking: Mimicking is copying the speech and actions of someone.
took to their heels: When people **take to their heels**, they run away quickly.

Comprehension

A. Complete the sentences with words from the text.

1. Sam wound up the Cro-Magnon Man but ______________________________
2. Sam froze with fear when ______________________________
3. Sam's mother was proud of ______________________________
4. The visiting human beings planned to ______________________________
5. The woman screamed and the man turned pale because ______________________________
6. Sam was surprised because ______________________________

B. Answer these questions.

1. What was the Cro-Magnon Man? Describe it briefly.
2. Why has the author described the cobwebs as 'designer cobwebs'? What other ornaments do you think Sam's mother would have decorated her house with?
3. 'If he had ears, he would not have believed them.' Explain this statement.
4. What tourist value did Sam's house have?
5. Why did Sam feel miserable when he heard his house was going to be pulled down?
6. How was the matter resolved? Describe in detail.

7. 'It was a rather nice feeling.' Explain this sentence.
8. What would you have done had you been in Sam's place?
9. Is this story a scary ghost story or a humorous one? Give reasons for your answer.

Vocabulary

A. Find the adjectives from the story that the writer has used to describe Sam's house as a spooky haunted ruin.

1. ________________ haveli
2. ________________ iron gates
3. ________________ drive
4. ________________ summerhouse
5. ________________ cobwebs

B. Find adjectives from the story that mean the same as these phrases.

1. created by an expert ________________
2. impressive and splendid ________________
3. fearless ________________
4. that which is shaky and can fall ________________
5. that moves like a machine ________________

C. Complete the sentences with these words. The first letter of each word is given.

said	boomed	growl	shriek	tell

1. It is s____________ that a dog is a man's best friend.
2. The familiar voice of his father b____________ in his ears.

3. The tiger let out a g____________ and attacked the hunters.
4. A s________________ woke me from my sleep.
5. Our grandmother used to t________________ us many tales every night.

Activity

Write the autobiography of the Cro-Magnon Man, using the hints given below.

- he was born how many years ago
- how he died and became a skeleton
- how he came to be in the possession of the Spooks
- how he loved to play with Sam
- how he frightened the human beings
- how he felt about it

SUGGESTIONS FOR FURTHER READING

- ***The Canterville Ghost***: This story by Oscar Wilde is a humorous account of the numerous attempts made by the ghost of a nobleman, Sir Simon, to frighten an American family that comes to live in a British mansion.
- ***Dial a Ghost***: This story by Eva Ibbotson is about the Wilkinson family that lived happily through World War II in England till their house is bombed and they all become homeless ghosts. The story narrates how they adjust to a ghostly life and how they 'live' for decades.

11

Wind Song

LILIAN MOORE

There is silence all around us, but when the wind begins to blow, all natural and man-made objects create a sound that becomes the song of the wind. The wind brings out the music in our hearts.

When the wind blows
The quiet things speak.[1]
Some whisper, some **clang**,[2]
Some creak.[3]

Grasses **swish**[4]
Tree tops **sigh**[5]
Flags **slap**[6]
And snap[7] at the sky.
Wires on poles
Whistle and hum.[8]
Trash cans roll.
Windows drum.[9]

When the wind goes—
Suddenly then,
the quiet things
are quiet again.

clang: Clang is a loud, ringing sound of metal hitting against something.

swish: Swish is a soft sweeping or brushing sound.

sigh: When you **sigh**, you take a deep breath that can be heard.

slap: (here) **Slap** is a noise like that of a slap.

LITERARY TERMS

2, 3, 4, 5, 6, 7, 8 & 9 are examples of **onomatopoeia**. The pronunciation of these words is the same as the sound they represent.

1, 4, 5, 7, 8 & 9 are examples of **personification**. All of them are non-living things that have been attributed with qualities of human beings.

ABOUT THE POET

Lilian Moore (1909-2004) was a teacher and a reading specialist. She helped to make children's books more affordable. Her works of poetry include *I Feel the Same Way, I Thought I Heard the City, Sam's Place: Poems from the Country, See My Lovely Poison Ivy, Think of Shadows* and *Something New Begins.*

Comprehension

A. Read the lines and answer the questions that follow.

1. *When the wind blows*

   The quiet things speak.

   1. What does the poet mean by saying 'quiet things speak'?
   2. What happens when the wind does not blow?

2. *Flags slap*

   And snap at the sky.

   Wires on poles

   Whistle and hum.

   1. How do you think flags 'snap' and 'slap'?
   2. Which wires is the poet referring to?
   3. What sounds do they make and how?

3. *Suddenly then,*

   the quiet things

   are quiet again.

   1. When do quiet things become quiet again?

B. Answer the questions.

1. Does the poem start with sound or with silence? How does it end?
2. What happens in the poem?
3. What are the different sound words that the poet has used?
4. Name three quiet things that 'speak' in the poem.
5. What kind of wind would be required to make a trash can roll and make the noise of a 'drumming' window?
6. What do you prefer more—sound or silence?

The language of poetry

A. Match the sounds with the things or animals that make that sound.

Sounds	Animals/Objects
1. buzz	a. thunder
2. squelch	b. leaves
3. rumble	c. sound of walking through mud
4. rustle	d. bees
5. roar	e. fire
6. crackle	f. cannon
7. boom	g. birds
8. splash	h. lion
9. twitter	i. water

Personification means using human qualities or actions to describe an object or an animal. For example,

Stars danced across the sky.

The wind howled in the night.

The car complained as the key was turned.

B. Now read the poem given below and underline the examples of personification. How many examples of personification are there in this poem?

It's Spring

It's spring
And the garden is changing its clothes,
Putting away
Its dark winter suits,
Its dull scarves
And drab brown overcoats.

Now, it wraps itself in green shoots,
Slips on blouses
Sleeved with pink and white blossom,
Pulls on skirts of daffodil and primrose,
Snowdrop socks and purple crocus shoes,
Then dances in the sunlight.

– John Foster

Activity

Imagine you are the wind. As you begin to blow, you touch and speak to all the quiet things mentioned in the poem.

As the wind, what do you say to them when they are quiet and when they begin to 'speak'?

If you want, you can add more quiet things that 'speak' when the wind blows.

SUGGESTIONS FOR FURTHER READING

- ***The Wind***: This poem by R. L. Stevenson is written from a child's point of view. It describes the actions caused by the blowing of the wind, which keeps itself hidden from human eyes.
- ***A Year's Windfalls***: This is a poem by Christina Rossetti. A 'seasonal' poem, it describes the kinds of winds that blow in different months and the effects they create.

12

The Bird with the Broken Wing

FLORENCE HOLBROOK

People who are kind and helpful are always loved and popular. Why are some trees evergreen and why do others lose their leaves during fall? This play attempts to give some answers.

Characters

The Bird
The Willow
The Juniper
The Oak Tree
The Spruce
The Forest Fairy
The Maple
The Pine
Jack Frost

Scene I—In the Woods

The Oak: See that flock of birds coming! The winter is near and they are flying south.

The Maple: I hope they will not **light on** my branches; I like to keep my leaves in order.

light on: To **light on** something is to sit on it.

The Willow: So many birds will break my **tender** twigs. I am sure I do not want them either. Here they come!

(*The birds fly over the trees.*)

Little Bird: Oh, I can fly no farther! My wing is broken. I am so tired and cold and hungry! I must rest tonight in this forest.

I am sure some big strong tree will give me a resting place. I will ask this tall Oak, he looks so strong and his leaves are so thick and warm! May I rest in your branches tonight, great Oak Tree? I am a poor little bird with a broken wing and I am cold and tired and hungry.

The Oak: I am sorry; but my branches are all **engaged** by the squirrels, who are getting their **acorns** in for the winter. I have no room for strange birds.

Little Bird: Oh! I am so lonely, so tired! Surely the handsome Maple Tree will take me in. Kind, lovely Maple Tree, may I rest tonight in your branches? I am a poor little bird with a broken wing. I will not harm your pretty leaves.

The Maple: My leaves tremble to think of taking in strange birds! My house is in perfect order and I cannot think of disturbing it. Please, go away!

Little Bird: Oh, what shall I do? The Oak and the Maple are so unkind. Surely some tree must be kind. Dear Willow, will you take me upon your graceful branches just for tonight?

The Willow: Really, Mr Bird, I think you should have gone on with the other birds. I cannot take you in. I do not know your name or anything about you. So, good night!

Little Bird: Oh, my dear bird friends, how I wish some of you were here! I shall **perish** with the cold. The Oak, the Maple, and the Willow have all turned me away.

The Spruce: Dear little bird, come to me! Can you hop up into my branches if I hold them down for you? I am not as handsome as

tender: Something that is **tender** is soft and weak.
engaged: When someone is **engaged** by something, he/she is involved in some activity.
acorn: An **acorn** is the fruit of an oak tree.
perish: To **perish** is to die or get killed.

the Maple tree, but my leaves grow thick and I'll try to keep you warm through the night.

Little Bird: Dear Spruce tree, how kind you are! Yes, here I am, on your lowest branch. How cosy and warm I feel. Oh, you are so good. I wish I could ever thank you for your goodness.

The Spruce: Do not speak of that, dear little bird; I am ashamed of the proud, selfish trees that would not shelter you. Should we not all be kind and helpful to one another?

The Pine: Well said, sister Spruce. And I will do my best to help you. I will stand between you and the cold north wind.

Little Bird: I thank you, tall Pine tree. You are a good brother of the Spruce.

The Juniper: I cannot keep the strong north wind from you, little bird, but if you are hungry, you may eat some of my berries. Perhaps, then, you will rest better.

Little Bird: Thank you, dear Juniper tree. Your berries are good and now I am cold and hungry no longer. I'll go to sleep. Good night, dear trees!

Trees: Good night, little bird, and may you have sweet dreams!

SCENE II—Midnight in the Forest

Jack Frost: Here I am in the great forest. How I dislike to touch all these beautiful leaves; yet I must obey the orders of King Winter. Here comes the Forest Fairy. Do you know why I have come, dear Fairy of the Forest?

Forest Fairy: Yes, Mr Frost. I know that you must touch all the leaves, turning them into brilliant **hues** of gold and crimson and brown. I dislike to have them go, and yet you and I must obey the commands of King Winter. But ...

Jack Frost: But what, dear Fairy? You speak as if you had some wish to make ...

Forest Fairy: I must tell you. A dear little bird came to the forest this evening. He had a broken wing, and he was cold and very tired. He asked shelter from the great Oak, the proud Maple, and the graceful Willow, and they all refused. I was so ashamed of my trees!

Jack Frost: What! Did all the trees refuse to help a poor, tired little bird?

Forest Fairy: Listen! Just as I was intending to speak to the trees, I heard the Spruce tell him to come to her branches and she would give him **shelter**. Then, the Pine tree offered to keep the north wind from him, and the Juniper gave him her berries to eat. Could you, dear Jack Frost ...

---

hue: A **hue** is a shade of a colour.
shelter: A **shelter** is a covered place where one can be safe from danger.

Jack Frost: Yes, yes, I know what you would ask. Such kindness as this should meet with some reward. The leaves of the proud Oak, the Maple, and the Willow shall fall to the ground when the cold of winter comes; but the Spruce, the Pine, the Juniper, and all their family shall keep their leaves and they shall be green all through the year. They shall be called the evergreen trees.

ABOUT THE AUTHOR

Florence Holbrook (1897- 1932) was an author and educator, belonging to Chicago. Her most popular book is *Book of Nature Myths for Children* in which she has collected 54 nature myths from around the world and retold them for young readers.

Comprehension

A. Choose the correct answer.

1. The trees were worried because
   a. a storm was brewing.
   b. a woodcutter was approaching them.
   c. it was winter and the birds were flying south.

2. The little bird could not fly any further because
   a. its wing was broken.
   b. it was very hot.
   c. it was lost.
3. Jack Frost had come to the forest because
   a. he wished to meet the trees.
   b. he wanted to help the little bird.
   c. he had to fulfill King Winter's orders that the trees must lose their leaves as winter approached.
4. The Forest Fairy felt ashamed of the trees because
   a. they refused to help the little bird.
   b. they fought with each other.
   c. they did not have any flowers.

B. Match the following.

Tree	Excuse offered for not helping the bird
1. Maple	a. did not want to give shelter to an unknown bird
2. Oak	b. did not want to disturb its tender twigs and pretty leaves
3. Willow	c. its branches were engaged by squirrels gathering acorns

C. Match the following.

Tree	Help offered
1. Pine	a. will keep the bird warm with its thick leaves
2. Spruce	b. offered its berries
3. Juniper	c. will protect the bird from the cold winds

B. Answer these questions.

1. Why do many birds fly South in winters?
2. The Oak, the Maple and the Willow are symbols of certain kind of people. Whom do they represent?
3. How were the Spruce, the Juniper and the Pine different from the other trees?
4. If you had been the Forest Fairy, would you have made the same wish as she did? Why?
5. Jack Frost punished the Oak, the Maple and the Willow. Was it a just punishment?
6. The play tries to teach its readers a lesson. What is the lesson?

Vocabulary

A. Write down the word which is being described in the meaning.

Sentence	Meaning	Word
1. He was a thin, rather handsome man in a smart uniform.	good looking	
2. Her dance was graceful, coordinated and a pleasure to watch.	elegant and charming	
3. More immigrants settle in California than in other parts of the US.	person who moves to a new country to make his/her home there	

4. The actions of his rebellious brother caused him to feel ashamed.	to feel inferior to someone else	
5. He does not understand that his selfish acts annoy others.	being focused only on oneself	

B. Given below are phrasal verbs from the play. Use them to complete the sentences.

stand between turned someone away offered something to fall to taking in

1. He ____________________ the beggar from his door without a penny.

2. Now that nobody is willing to run this errand, it ____________________ me.

3. The polite young man ____________________ the chair ____________________ the senior citizen.

4. The landlord is not averse to ____________________ tenants.

5. We wish all success; we will not ____________________ you and your goals.

Activity

Imagine you are the little bird with the broken wing.

A TV journalist comes to know about your story and takes your interview. Write down the questions asked by the journalist and the answers given by the you.

You can ask these kinds of questions:

- What happened?
- Where did it happen?

- How did it happen?
- Why did it happen?
- How did you feel?

SUGGESTIONS FOR FURTHER READING

- ***Time and the Seasons***: This is a short play by Florence Holbrook. In it, Father Time summons his daughters, the four seasons, and gives them orders for what to do for the New Year.
- ***The Blue Bird***: This is a play by Maurice Maeterlinck. In the play, Mytyl and her brother Tyltyl, woodchopper's children, go on a magical trip to look for happiness represented by the Blue Bird of Happiness. They are helped by the Fairy Berylune and are accompanied by a dog, a cat, Light, Fire and Bread.

Literary Genres

Horror is a type of story or a piece of writing which scares or startles the reader. A horror story creates a frightening atmosphere and often has supernatural themes and characters, like ghosts, witches or vampires.

Literary Terms

Onomatopoeia is the use of words whose pronunciation is similar to the sounds they represent. For example, *honk, bang, buzz*

Personification is a way of imagining non-living things or abstract ideas as human beings with thoughts, actions and emotions. For example, *The moon danced over the water.*

NOTES

NOTES